Where Animals Live

S0-ALF-117

The World of Penguins

Adapted from Doug Allan's *The Penguin in the Snow*

**Words by
David Saintsing**

**Photographs by
Doug Allan**

Oxford Scientific Films

Gareth Stevens Publishing
Milwaukee

Contents

Note: The use of a capital letter for a penguin's name means that it is a specific *type* (or *species*) of penguin (such as the Macaroni Penguin). The use of a lower case, or small, letter for a penguin's name means that it is a member of the larger *group* of penguins.

Where Penguins Live

Penguins are sea birds that cannot fly. They are well-suited for a life at sea. Some spend up to five months at sea. These Adelie Penguins are walking over the frozen sea in Antarctica.

There are 18 different *species* of penguins, and they are only found south of the *equator*. Penguins are best adapted for cool places, usually near and in Antarctica. But some, like these Jackass Penguins, live in warmer coastal areas of South Africa, Australia, and New Zealand.

3

Penguins in Antarctica

Penguins like to stay in large groups, even when they swim at sea. They keep together by calling to each other. This helps them find food and guard against *predators*.

When penguins are on shore, they gather in groups called *rookeries*. There may be thousands or even millions of penguins in a rookery! In Antarctica, the rookery is often on barren frozen ground or snow.

During the summer the ice breaks up in Antarctica. Then the penguins can swim and fish close to their rookeries.

As the sea freezes over in the winter, the penguins *migrate* north. Now they can stay close to open water for feeding. Sometimes they migrate as far as 500 miles (800 km).

Penguins spend their lives both at sea and on land. These two different *environments* present them with many challenges.

Polar Penguins and Their Rookeries

In the summer, the south polar seas are full of penguins near their rookeries. Often sailors can smell the *guano* far out at sea. Sometimes penguins are seen standing on the ice *floes* that bob in the sea even in the summer.

Penguins must be able to reach the sea easily. Therefore, rookeries cannot be near steep cliffs. Penguins like gently sloping rocky shores. Here, they can easily reach water and find pebbles for their nests.

Good places for rookeries are hard to find in icy Antarctica, and penguins often occupy every spot in their rookery. When weather and other conditions are good, there may be over one million penguins in a rookery.

Penguins nest together in their rookeries. But there is always some space between nests. Penguins defend their little territories against other penguins in the rookery.

The Penguin's Body

Penguins don't look like most birds you know! Only when you look closely do you see that they are covered with feathers. Their short wings have *evolved* into paddles, and their bodies are streamlined for swimming.

Like all birds, penguins are warm-blooded. To keep warm, they have thick *plumage*. Beneath the outer feathers is a layer of *down*. This traps warm air like a coat. There is also a layer of fat under the skin for more insulation.

Flying birds have light bones. But the penguin has developed heavy bones in the *flippers* for swimming and fighting.

All penguins have dark backs and light fronts. This *camouflage* makes penguins hard to see in the water.

Like the Chinstrap (above), Macaroni (left), and King Penguins (right), penguins often have different head markings. These help the different breeds recognize each other. They also help the penguins stay together at sea.

Movement in Water and on Land

Penguins are excellent swimmers. If you go to a zoo, you can see how their flippers beat up and down like wings to push the penguins through the water.

When traveling at sea, penguins move by "porpoising." They swim underwater and jump out, like a porpoise, to breathe every 15 seconds or so. Penguins can reach speeds of 20 mph (32 kph) by porpoising. Sometimes they swim hundreds of miles (km) in their winter journeys.

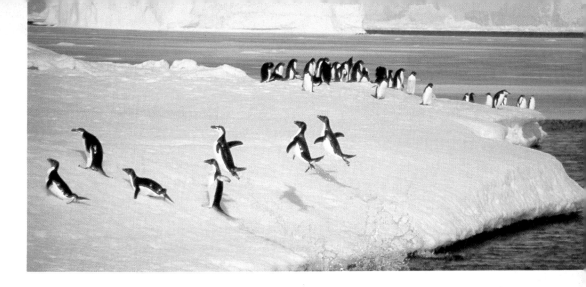

In some places where penguins come ashore there are little ice cliffs at the water's edge. To come ashore, penguins swim very deep and then swim to the surface very quickly. They then shoot out of the water and onto the ice.

On icy shores or frozen seas, penguins travel by walking or by "tobogganing." This means that they drop onto their bellies and slide quickly across the ice.

Feeding

Penguins always feed at sea. In polar regions there is a large supply of *"krill."* Krill is a small shrimp-like animal that lives in huge swarms. Penguins also feed on fish and squid.

Large Emperor Penguins dive as deep as 800 ft (250 m) for food, and they can stay underwater for as long as 20 minutes. When diving, their heartbeat slows down so oxygen in the blood lasts longer. These Adelies (below) are entering the sea on a feeding trip.

Penguins have fleshy spines on their tongues to hold their slippery *prey*. Penguins feed their young by passing food from their stomach to their chicks on shore. They have large stomachs, so they can eat a lot far out at sea and still have food for the chicks when they return.

A Penguin can eat fish much bigger than it can swallow. Its beak and throat stretch to take in these large meals.

Staying Cool and Keeping Clean

Even in a world of snow and ice, penguins sometimes get too warm. They can stay cool by eating snow or drinking extra water. If there is a breeze, they will stretch out their flippers and fluff out their feathers. This helps give off heat.

Each year penguins replace all their feathers. This is called *molting*. For 3-4 weeks, penguins do not feed or go to sea. They live off the fat stored in their bodies.

↑

To keep their feathers in good shape, penguins spend lots of time *preening*. Penguins produce a special oil in a *gland* near the tail. They spread this oil around with their beaks to keep their feathers healthy and waterproof.

Courtship and Mating

Spring comes to Antarctica in October. This is when penguins start to return to their rookeries. The males arrive first. They often make their nest in the same spot from year to year. They may add new stones and some moss to the nest. The nests keep the eggs from rolling away.

Penguins often have the same mates from year to year. They may have separated over the winter. But they know each other by their mating displays. The male attracts the female by raising his head, flapping his flippers, and squawking. In large rookeries, it often sounds as if each penguin is trying to shout louder than the others! Sometimes two males will argue over the same nest (below) or female.

The male fertilizes the eggs inside the female's body. About 3-4 days after the first egg is laid, the second follows.

Incubation and Hatching

Both parents take turns *incubating* the eggs. The first egg is kept cooler so it hatches at the same time as the second.

Penguins have a bare patch of skin called a *broodpouch* (above). When the parents settle down on an egg, it is kept off the ground by the feet. It is then pulled into the broodpouch. The eggs can be kept very warm this way, even in a blizzard.

Because of predators, penguins never leave their eggs unattended. When one parent returns from the sea after feeding, it takes over incubating the eggs from the other.

Incubation takes about 35 days. The parents know when the chicks are ready to hatch because they can hear chirping inside the eggs. The babies peck themselves out using the "egg tooth." As soon as the babies are hatched, the parents tuck them into the broodpouch.

From Hatching to Fledging

Baby penguins like to run around the rookery, where they can get very dirty (below). But they become cold very easily, so during the first week they stay in the brood pouch, where it is warm. They only show themselves when they want to be fed. When they are hungry, they peck at the parent's beak. The parent leans over, and the baby gets its food right from inside the parent's mouth!

The babies grow very quickly. As they grow, their appetite also grows, and both parents must go out to sea to catch enough food. Some adults stay in the rookery to protect the babies. Each adult feeds only its own chicks.

After six weeks, the baby penguins begin to *fledge.* They lose their fluffy down and, like these chicks, they begin to look like adults. Soon they will hunt their own food at sea.

The Family Life of Emperor Penguins

Emperors, the largest penguins, are about 4 ft (1.2 m) tall and weigh around 70 lbs (30 kg). Emperor chicks stay in their rookeries for four months instead of the usual two for other types of penguins. This Emperor chick has just hatched. It stays warm by sitting on its parent's feet and staying in the broodpouch. ↓

Emperors make their rookeries on the frozen seas. They lay a single egg and do not build nests. The eggs rest on the feet and in the broodpouch of the males to stay warm. Antarctica is dark all the time in the middle of winter, and it's very cold. The males stand close together to help keep warm. They incubate the eggs for two months and live off the fat in their bodies.

The females go off to feed where the seas are not frozen. They return to care for the newly hatched chicks.

Enemies and Defense

Leopard Seals are the main enemies of penguins at sea. The seals stay near the rookeries and hunt the penguins as they come and go to feed. The young penguins are at risk the most. They tire easily as the seals chase them in the water.

Penguins are generally safe from predators on land. Only sick or weak adult penguins are attacked by large sea birds. Healthy adults can defend themselves.

↑

Penguin eggs and chicks are in danger on land, however. Skuas work in pairs to distract the parents and then come in to take the eggs.

Sheathbills watch until penguin chicks are being fed. They then scare the chicks so their food drops on the ground. The Sheathbills then steal the food for their own chicks.

↓

Penguins and People

In the early days of voyages to south polar seas, humans were a danger to penguins. Some people would take the eggs or kill the adults for food. Today, people are interested in saving penguins. This scientist is weighing a Chinstrap.

Scientists work to protect the rookeries and leave the penguins undisturbed. They count the penguins carefully, using paint to be sure they only count each penguin once. Some penguins are actually increasing in number.

Right now, there is little danger of *pollution* where polar penguins live. Oil has been discovered there, however. If drilling begins, safety steps must be taken to prevent oil spills. Spills might poison penguins and damage their protective plumage.

Recently, people in special fishing boats have begun harvesting krill from the seas for food. Some people worry that not enough krill will be left for penguins. Countries have agreed to limit the krill they catch.

Friends and Neighbors

On land, this Southern Fur Seal (above) visits a rookery — and a curious Chinstrap chick! Other seals, such as this Weddell Seal (below right), also share beaches with penguins.

The huge amounts of krill that attract penguins to the seas also appeal to whales. Whales, the world's biggest animals, can be up to 100 ft (30 m) long. And like penguins, they swallow krill less than 3 inches (8 cm) long.

Different kinds of penguins sometimes nest together. But they are very noisy, and the rookery is crowded and dirty. Therefore, other birds, such as Sheathbills, nest mostly under ledges that are too low for penguins. Or, like petrels and cormorants, they nest on cliffs overlooking the rookery.

Life in the Snow

Many animals feed on the same food that penguins eat. And some also feed on penguins themselves. Penguins are thus part of the south polar food chain. As this food chain picture shows, penguins do not have that many predators, and those that are eaten by other animals are often weakened by disease or injury.

Food Chain

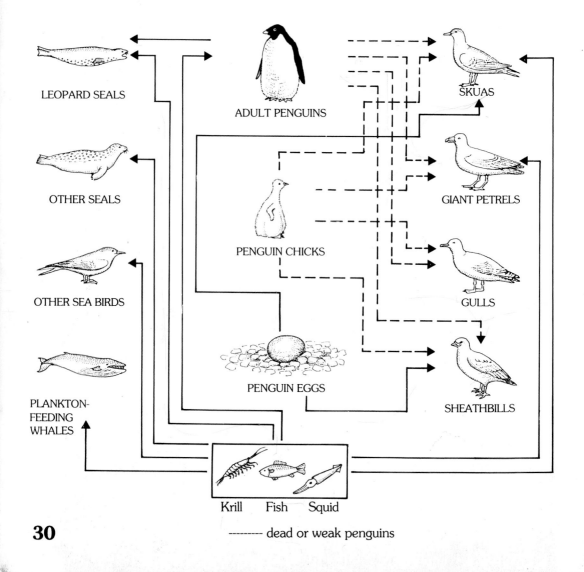

LEOPARD SEALS

ADULT PENGUINS

SKUAS

OTHER SEALS

PENGUIN CHICKS

GIANT PETRELS

OTHER SEA BIRDS

GULLS

PLANKTON-
FEEDING
WHALES

PENGUIN EGGS

SHEATHBILLS

Krill   Fish   Squid

-------- dead or weak penguins

Penguins are nicely suited for life in the south polar region. They can live a very long time. Adelies (above) can live up to 12 years, and Emperors (below) can live up to 20. Penguins live where there are few people, so there is little pollution. As we begin to use Antarctica, however, we must be careful not to spoil the *habitat* of those tough little birds, the penguins.

Index and New Words About Penguins

These new words about penguins appear in the text on the pages shown after each definition. Each new word first appears in the text in *italics*, just as it appears here.

Reading level analysis: SPACHE 2.4, FRY 2-3, FLESCH 91 (very easy), RAYGOR 3-4, FOG 4-5, SMOG 3

Library of Congress Cataloging-in-Publication Data
Saintsing, David.
The world of penguins.
(Where animals live)
"Adapted from Doug Allan's The penguin in the snow."
Includes index.
Summary: Text and photographs describe the lives of penguins, including their feeding, breeding, and defense behavior.
1. Penguins--Juvenile literature. [1. Penguins] I. Allan, Douglas. The penguin in the snow. II. Oxford Scientific Films. III. Title. IV. Series.
QL696.S473S25 1988   598.4'41   87-6536
ISBN 1-55532-299-9   ISBN 1-55532-274-3 (lib. bdg.)

North American edition first published in 1988 by
Gareth Stevens, Inc.
7221West Green Tree Road Milwaukee, WI 53223, USA
US edition, this format, copyright © 1988 by Belitha Press Ltd.
Text copyright © 1988 by Gareth Stevens, Inc.

Typeset in Milwaukee by Web Tech, Inc. Printed in the United States of America.
Series Editor: Mark J. Sachner. Art Director: Treld Bicknell.
Design: Naomi Games. Cover Design: Gary Moseley. Line Drawings: Lorna Turpin.
Scientific Consultants: Gwynne Vevers and David Saintsing.

The publishers wish to thank the following for permission to reproduce copyright photographs: **Doug Allan** for front cover, title page, and back cover; pp. 3, 4, 5, 6, 7, 9 all, 10, 11 both, 12, 13, 14, 15 both, 16 both, 17, 18 both, 19, 20 all, 22 both, 23, 24, 25 both, 26 both, 28, 29 both, and 31 both. **Oxford Scientific Films Ltd.** for p. 2 (photographer David Curl); p. 8 (photographer Andrew Lister); p. 27 (photographer E.C.G. Lemon).

2 3 4 5 6 7 8 9 93 92 91 90 89